KT-503-778

THEY DIED TOO YOUNG

JAMES DEAN

BY
A. Noble

This edition first published by Parragon Books Ltd in 1995

Produced by
Magpie Books Ltd

Copyright © Parragon Book Service Ltd 1995
Unit 13–17, Avonbridge Trading Estate, Atlantic Road
Avonmouth,
Bristol
BS11 9QD

Illustrations courtesy of Rex Features

ISBN 0 75250 169 0

A copy of the British Library Cataloguing in Publication
Data is available from the British Library.

Typeset by Hewer Text Composition Services, Edinburgh
Printed in Singapore by Printlink International Co.

James Dean is one of the icons of the late twentieth century, up there with Marilyn Monroe and Marlon Brando. This may seem curious, as he starred in only three films, *East of Eden*, *Rebel Without a Cause* and *Giant*, whereas Monroe and Brando have many films to their name. But, just as Brando caught the new spirit of youthful rebelliousness in *The Wild Ones*, so James Dean embodied the feeling of so many teenagers, that of uncertainty as they approached adulthood and its challenges. And the 1950s, when the word 'teenager' was coined, was the decade in which people of this age group were recognized as having concerns (and money) of their own, which the entertainment industry, especially in Hollywood, and with music, began to express and exploit. Youth culture, as it is now known, had arrived and has been with us ever since.

BIRTH OF A REBEL

James Byron Dean was born on 8 February 1931 in Fairmount, Indiana, in 'Hoosier' country, as Indiana is known. Indiana is real middle America, farming land, with no industry and little culture – there was not even a cinema in Fairmount, as it had closed down due to lack of interest from the local Quaker folk. Jimmy Dean's parents were both local, from families that had farmed in the area for generations. His father, Winton Dean, was the first to break away from his farming heritage and had become a dental technician. His mother, Mildred Wilson, had married Winton after a brief courtship when she discovered she was pregnant.

Initially the family rented rooms in a house called the Seven Gables Apartment, but then they moved to a cottage on Back Creek, a small stream that ran behind Marcus Winslow's farm. Winslow was Winton Dean's brother-in-law, married to his sister Ortense. Mildred spent much of her time with Jimmy, and he was if anything a spoilt child, never wanting for toys despite his parents' slender means.

And his mother showed her over-whelming affection for him by read-ing poetry and the classics, and putting on playlets with her son. This was the start of Jimmy's lifelong interest in culture.

When Jimmy was five, his father was transferred to the Sawtelle Veterans Administration in Los Angeles and the family moved to Santa Monica, where Mildred managed to find en-ough money for violin lessons for her little boy. But the family idyll was not to last. When Jimmy was nine years old, his mother developed cancer of the uterus. X-rays showed it to be well advanced. On 14 July 1940, she died with her husband and son at her bedside. Her corpse was transported back to Fairmount, with Jimmy and his grandmother travelling on the same train Her body lay in the Winslows' house for two days for relatives to pay their last respects, and as a memento Jimmy cut off a lock of her hair.

Winton was unable to leave his job in Los Angeles and asked if anyone from his extensive family could look after Jimmy. Marcus and Ortense volunteered; they had a fourteen-old daughter, Jean, but had always wanted a son. Jimmy knew the Winslows well, having been a neighbour in earlier childhood; it was Marcus who had taught him to fish. But he greatly missed his mother, keeping the lock of her hair under his pillow. Marcus was a kind surrogate father, turning a barn into a sort of gym and setting up lights on Back Creek so that Jimmy and his schoolfriends could play ice-hockey. The Winslows were conservative, God-fearing folk and brought Jimmy up to follow their beliefs.

Jimmy was adventurous as a child, and continued to be so throughout his short life. Despite his very short sight, he was given to trying tricks on the trapeze, one of which broke four of his front teeth; he also rode a bull at a country fair. Also his talent for imitating people, both physically and verbally came out at an early age. Ortense recognized his talent and put him in for reading competitions, at several of which he won prizes. But he could be wilful, and when he didn't want to perform he wouldn't, which sometimes embarrassed the Winslows. He was, it seems, something of a troublemaker, being competitive and unruly, perhaps seeking the attention he had lost with his mother's death.

Marcus Winslow gave him a moped for his thirteenth birthday, and with this machine Jimmy began an affair with speed that was eventually to kill him. He traded in the moped as soon as possible for a motorcycle and soon began pushing it to its limit. Apparently, though, he never had an accident, despite the tricks he performed and this made him extremely fearless. He also became something of an expert daredevil driver using cars owned by his schoolmates, and spent a lot of time hanging out at the local garage, Marvin Carter's Cycles, with other enthusiasts. Despite being short, and short-sighted, he managed to get into the school basketball team – as prestigious as being in a school first XI in Britain, which shows how determined he was. He also took up pole vaulting and established a county record when he was seventeen. Once he had achieved this, he gave it up. He was always out to prove himself.

But home life at the farm became increasingly dull, and the Winslows found that Jimmy was moving away from them in his ideas and aspirations. He developed an infatuation for Dr James DeWeerd, a wounded war hero, a man who had travelled abroad, and who was now pastor of the Wesleyan Church in Fairmount. As an educated and relatively cultured man, he deeply impressed Jimmy – he was so different from the homely farm folks. He introduced Jimmy to the world of ideas, and also to the world of homosexuality. DeWeerd liked to encourage local youths to swim naked in the local YMCA pool, but with Jimmy he went further, first of all letting him feel his war wounds and then engaging in further intimacies. To some extent, he used his position as a pastor to prey on Jimmy's guilt over the death of his mother, persuading him that he was depraved and evil. To balance his uncertainty over his masculinity Jimmy began an affair with a school PE teacher, Betty

McPherson. He must have found life quite confusing.

Before leaving school he managed to get into the national reading finals of the National Forensic League competition, a great achievement for someone from Fairmount – it was even reported in the *Fairmount News*. He hadn't even told the Winslows that he had entered the competition. Typically, though the contestants were expected to declaim in jacket and tie, Jimmy appeared in an open shirt and jeans. During preparation he was teased by his classmates about his acting ability – they probably didn't think much of acting as something one would want to be good at. Jimmy became involved in a fight, which

James Dean

Marcus Wilson's farm in Fairmount, Indiana

the headmaster happened on; he was temporarily expelled.

During his time at school, Jimmy appeared in virtually all the plays that were put on; in these he made a great impression, especially on his relatives. The time came for him to leave, though, and against Marcus Winslow's wishes, Winton Dean decided that Jimmy should study in California. Because his grades were not that good, Jimmy wasn't eligible for UCLA (University of California at Los Angeles), so it was decided that he would spend a term at Santa Monica College to prepare. This move, given Jimmy's desire to be an actor, suited him down to the ground. In June 1949 he headed off for Los Angeles.

Los Angeles

Jimmy went to live with his father, and his second wife, Ethel Case. Any fears that Jimmy might not be able to get on with his stepmother proved unfounded, as Jimmy always related well to older women. His father's attempts to make up for his long absence from Jimmy's life were not particularly successful; also they argued about his career. His father did not think Jimmy's dramatic success at the Fairmount school was significant, and persuaded his son to sign up for a law course. As a bribe he bought him a second-hand car. None the less, many drama options were offered at Santa Monica and Jimmy entered all such available courses.

Gene Owen was head of the college drama department and she was immediately impressed by Jimmy's talent. After a period at Santa Monica it became clear that Jimmy was not doing well in his law courses, but was in drama, and he was able to persuade a reluctant Winton that he should study drama at UCLA. He also became stage manager for a summer repertory company, the Miller Playhouse Theatre, and even had a small part in a musical, using the name 'Byron James'. He moved into a fraternity (collegiate living quarters) and in October, after a week of auditions for UCLA's major productions, Jimmy got the part of Malcolm in *Macbeth*.

His stay in the fraternity did not last long, as he was nearly drowned in the special initiation rites devised for him – his disdain for rowdy fraternity activities had earned him its dislike and he left it to move in with another drama student, Bill Bast. Bill found Jimmy a moody character, swinging unpredictably from cheerfulness to moroseness. But Jimmy also told him what drove him: 'I don't even want to be the best. I want to grow so tall that nobody can reach me. Not to prove anything, but just to go where you ought to go when you devote your whole life and all you are to one thing.'

Jimmy received his first paid work at this time, appearing in a Pepsi–Cola advertisement with several teenagers, some of whom would later appear in *Rebel Without a Cause*. This led to a small part in a TV episode of *Family Theater*, 'Hill Number One', a playlet with a religious theme. Jimmy's role was St John, one of the twelve disciples; the show was broadcast on Easter Sunday 1951, and as it was compulsory viewing for a certain Catholic girls' school, Jimmy acquired his first fan club, the

Immaculate Heart James Dean Appreciation Society!

But like many aspiring actors, he was mostly out of work, and ended up doing odd jobs such as car parking at the CBS radio station. Because he refused to wear a jacket and tie and disliked taking orders, he had lost a job inside the studio. He also lost his flatmate, as he dumped his current girlfriend and started dating Bill Bast's. They had formed a regular foursome until then, and this was not part of the deal. It was typical of Jimmy's capacity to destroy relationships.

Soon after this, Jimmy was unable to pay the rent on the flat and had to move in with another friend. Shortly thereafter, while parking cars at CBS he met Rogers Brackett, an advertising executive who directed his own shows, and who was part of the Hollywood homosexual scene. Jimmy then moved in with Brackett, who got him work on radio shows, and one-liner roles in Sam Fuller's film *Fixed Bayonets*, and in the Dean Martin/Jerry Lewis film *Sailor Beware*. This wasn't enough for an ambitious young actor, increasingly in despair about the quantity and quality of the work he was doing, and Jimmy left college to study under James Whitmore, film star and Broadway actor. Whitmore advised Jimmy that if he really wanted to learn acting he should go to New York and study under Elia Kazan, who ran the Actors' Studio.

New York

New York was an awesome, exciting place, with its multi-ethnic vitality, its bustle, its status as the cultural capital of North America, very different from the sprawling mess of Los Angeles and the backwoods of Indiana. Initially, Jimmy was overwhelmed by it, and spent much of his time in cinemas, watching films over and over again, including Marlon Brando's *The Men* and Montgomery Clift's *A Place in the*

James Dean arrived in New York in 1951

The director Elia Kazan in later life

Sun. These two actors were his idols, and he learnt much from them.

Jimmy's first job was as a dishwasher, but this didn't last too long. New York was the hub of television production in the 1950s and there was a constant demand for actors. Jimmy got an agent, Jane Deacy, and in November, two months after he had arrived, a job testing stunts on a show called *Beat the Clock*.

One of the great loves of Jimmy's life was classical music, and in New York he met Leonard and Adele Rosenman. Leonard Rosenman was a composer and musician, and his wife was an accomplished pianist. Jimmy attached himself to the couple, as they

represented the cultural and intellec-
tual side of life that he craved – he was
an avid reader of philosophy and the
classics, although not that diligent,
putting down books when he felt he
understood the gist, without finishing
them. He liked to be seen as bookish,
often walking around with volumes
under his arm. Similarly, when he
persuaded Leonard Rosenman to
teach him the piano, he did not have
the application to practise enough to
acquire any real skill.

Jimmy met and moved in with Elizabeth 'Dizzy' Sheridan, a dancer, but
the pair drifted apart when Rogers
Brackett moved to New York. Jimmy was completely broke and the lure
of rent-free living outweighed his

romance. Brackett was a useful contact though, and more work came
Jimmy's way in early 1952, with
several bit parts: at least they were
acting parts, though, rather than
stunts. But there was a downside to
his life with Brackett; he was very
much the junior partner, financially
dependent, and compelled to mix
with all Brackett's homosexual
friends, who lived an alien extrava-
gant life-style of which he could never
really become part. When Bill Bast
announced his imminent arrival in
New York, Jimmy moved into an
apartment with him and Dizzy,
though he still went to parties that
Brackett invited him to in the hope
of making useful contacts. One letter
to the Winslows begs for money so

that he could buy a suit to make himself presentable at these high-falu-tin parties.

In September 1952 Jimmy met Christine White, an aspiring actress who also wanted to sign up with the Actors' Studio. She had even typed up a scene to perform at her audition, and needed a partner. Jimmy had walked in at just the right time, and the two rehearsed the scene endlessly. Through Brackett, though, Jimmy had met Lemuel Ayers, a theatrical producer, who offered him a part in the stage play *See the Jaguar*, where he had to play a sixteen-year old naïf who has been totally cut off from the world by an over-protective mother. Apparently, the author, N. Richard Nash, thought Jimmy perfect for the role, that of someone totally lost in and confused by the world.

In November he finally auditioned for Elia Kazan, then at the height of his career as a director, discoverer of new talent – Marlon Brando, for one – and trainer in 'method' acting. Jimmy and Christine were accepted for the Actors' Studio. On 3 December 1952 *See the Jaguar* opened, and the entire cast went to Sardi's restaurant, a thespian tradition in New York, to await the reviews. Jimmy was delighted to be the centre of attention. Unfortunately the play was panned, despite some good words for his acting, and the play was withdrawn after five performances. This gave him more time to attend the Actors' Studio. Part of the training was to put on brief performances which were then subject to criticism by the other actors. Jimmy appeared but was unable to take this criticism and only performed once.

But *See the Jaguar* put some money in his pocket and enabled him to indulge his love of speed: he bought an Indian 500 motorcycle. He also began a tempestuous romance with a sixteen-year old aspirant actress, Barbara Glenn. More television roles came his way because of reviews of his performance in *See the Jaguar*, though he was often cast as a psychotic, which gives some idea of how directors saw him – moody and difficult. He thought himself above learning technique, and liked to play roles in his

James Dean made his name in *East of Eden*

The new Hollywood heart-throb

own way. But whatever his difficulties in rehearsal, he was generally regarded as excellent in performance, especially when he had to work with children, to whom he seemed drawn.

The next big stage part that Jimmy had was in an adaptation of André Gide's autobiographical novel *The Immoralist*, where Jimmy played Bachir, a devious North African houseboy who seduces a French archaeologist, thereby giving his alcoholic wife something of a surprise. The lead was played by Louis Jourdain, his wife by Geraldine Page, both well-known stars. Jimmy gave both directors, Herman Shumlin (sacked by producer Barry Rose during rehearsals) and Daniel Mann, nightmares, repeating his lines in his own way, regardless of the director's wishes, and ad libbing. However, after initial confrontation he got on well enough with Shumlin. The pre-Broadway performances were staged in Philadelphia, where they were very well received. In the audience one night was Paul Osborn, who was writing the screenplay for *East of Eden*. He was suitably impressed and recommended that Elia Kazan see the play when it moved to New York.

Jimmy himself wasn't that impressed by the play. He tried to switch to the lead role in another play, *End as a Man*, where the actors were on strike. The strike ended, but the lead actor, Ben Gazzara, was not particularly enamoured of Jimmy's lack of solidarity.

Previews of *The Immoralist* were not very well received by the critics; but on the first night the audience went wild, especially the gay element. When taking his bow, Jimmy curtsied instead which incensed Mann, who went backstage to tear him off a strip. Jimmy replied by giving two weeks' notice, extraordinary behaviour from a little-known actor with a major part in what looked like being a Broadway hit.

But perhaps his behaviour was not as outrageous as it seemed. Jimmy knew there was a chance of a role in *Battle Cry*, an upcoming Warner Brothers film. The casting director, William T. Orr, came to New York and was extremely impressed by Jimmy's audition (as he was with Paul Newman's and Walter Matthau's), but Jimmy didn't get the part. More important, though, Elia Kazan had attended a performance of *The Immoralist*. Not particularly impressed by Jimmy's performance, he none the less thought he might be right for the part of Cal in *East of Eden*, feeling that the other options, Marlon Brando and Mont-gomery Clift, didn't quite have the teenage angst he was looking for, the quality of lovable but difficult bad boy. Jimmy turned up for the interview in his usual jeans, despite knowing how important the role could be. Not much was said until Jimmy asked Kazan if he'd like a ride on his 'sickle', his motorbike. He then put Kazan through the seventh degree in

New York traffic. Kazan probably did not feel much affection for Jimmy at this point, but felt he had the qualities the part required; he sent him to see John Steinbeck, the author of the original novel. Steinbeck was unimpressed, calling him a 'snotty kid', but agreed with Kazan that he was right for the part. Kazan chose Jimmy because: 'He has a grudge against all fathers. He is vengeful; he has a sense of aloneness and of being persecuted . . . [and] is tremendously talented.' Shortly afterwards Jimmy got the call he was waiting for, and according to Christine White he was elated.

Jimmy also developed an interest in photography, after meeting Roy

Schatt, via his ex-girlfriend Arlene
Sachs. Schatt made a living from
photographing actors and actresses,
and Jimmy pursued this line, in a
'candid camera' vein, photographing
friends when they were unaware he
had his Leica on him. Schatt recognized Jimmy's ability to become the
focus of the lens, to pose without
posing, and to use the light to his
best advantage, important abilities for
any actor, but especially one who
would act in film. Schatt and Jimmy
became firm friends and they and
others would gather in Schatt's house
to listen to jazz and party. Jimmy often
played the bongo drums at some of
these sessions, as they were another of
his enthusiasms. He was desperate to
learn, to know more of the world, to

develop broader talents. But at the same time, he always wanted to push his luck to the limits. After an accident on his motorbike, just before leaving for Hollywood for his screen test, Leonard Rosenman asked him why he took such risks. Jimmy's reply was: 'Death is always there and I want to conquer it.'

Hollywood

Jimmy flew out to California with Elia Kazan, who had time to size up his protégé, visually if not psychologically, as Jimmy was taciturn. He also saw Jimmy briefly in the company of his father and could see that the tension between them made Jimmy ideal for the rebellious Cal.

When Jimmy arrived in Hollywood in 1954, it was just getting over a bad period. The old system where cinemas had to accept whatever Hollywood sent them – a sort of 'tied' system – had been broken up in 1948 by anti-trust legislation, television was becoming a growing threat as the era of the 'couch potato' arrived, and McCarthyism, the paranoiac fear of communists – 'reds under the bed' – had swept America, manifesting itself in its worst form in Hollywood, where the Blacklist, a real document, led to actors suddenly finding themselves out of work for no reason, with no right of appeal. But as the Korean War ended and McCarthy was exposed as a malicious humbug, Hollywood began to revive, determined to counter these threats to its existence. Television directors were hired, bringing with

them new ideas, and the big screen
was developed. The old Hollywood
staple diet of Westerns, gangster films
and biblical stories was replaced by
films that appealed more to the spirit
of the times. There was also a new
market developing; as the US econo-
my grew rapidly after the Second
World War, teenagers began to have
money. The entertainment industry,
recognizing this, began to cater for
their needs, making films to which
they could relate. Hence *East of Eden*.

The budget for *East of Eden* was large
by the standards of the day – $1, 600,
000 – as it was to be shot in Cinema-
Scope, a big-screen format, in colour.
None of the crew could believe that
Jimmy was to be the star – he was so

Jimmy Dean with his beloved Triumph
motorcycle

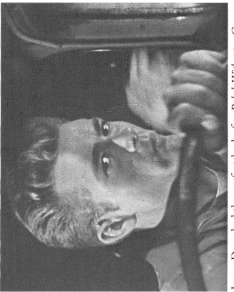

James Dean had the perfect looks for *Rebel Without a Cause*

unlike the stars they were used to. Warner made hard-bitten gangster movies with men like Cagney and Bogart in the lead roles. A scruffy, short, bespectacled youth was not what they had envisaged. Kazan put Jimmy in a flat with Dick Davalos, who played Cal's rival in the film. He thought that living with Jimmy would be enough to make Davalos dislike him, which would be good for their roles, and he was right!

Jimmy received $300 a week until the contract was signed – a sizeable income in 1954 – and he spent time before shooting began looking up old contacts in Santa Monica. But the reunions were not successful. Jimmy clearly thought that he had reached the peak of his profession and looked down on his old teachers and acquaintances, who quite quickly had had enough of him. The only person with whom he successfully resumed a relationship was Dick Clayton who had been in *Sailor Beware*, but who now was working as an agent, acting for Jimmy in Los Angeles. But much of the time Jimmy was by himself studying the script. He made no attempt to be amiable to the crew and they thought him pretty arrogant. Meanwhile Kazan went through the test footage of Jimmy and decided to sign him up for the princely sum of $1,000 a week. While Jimmy had not been particularly co-operative in front of the cameras, he had been natural.

Once signed, Jimmy was packed off to
Salinas, California, where much of the
film would be shot. He was put under
the tutelage of 'Monty' Roberts, who
was an expert rider and rodeo man,
and who had doubled for many actors
on horseback. Monty lived on a ranch
and Jimmy was sent there to get a feel
for life in the sticks in California and to
be fattened and toughened up. Kazan
thought he was too skinny to play a
farmboy, even though that is in fact
what Jimmy had been back in Indiana.
Within a month Jimmy was fully at
home, inseparable from Monty, and
able to reproduce the local accent; he
also understood the attitudes of local
people. He outwardly led a life of
bucolic cheer, but inwardly, as he
wrote to Barbara Glenn, he was near

38

despair; he didn't have his motorcycle with him and he didn't like the people, especially the girls, whom he clearly found mindless and boring. Consolation came when he returned to Los Angeles and bought a horse for $250, with which he said he had fallen in love!

He also bought himself a motorbike, a Triumph T-110, which he drove around the studio, much to the annoyance of Kazan, who was not keen on Jimmy's apparent death wish, nor the threat it posed to others working on the lot. Kazan banned Jimmy from riding the motorcycle until the film was finished, so Jimmy went off and bought himself an MG TA, to satisfy his lust for speed. With this machine he

With Natalie Wood in *Rebel Without a Cause*

Relaxing with his drum

managed to terrify one of his co-stars,
Julie Harris, whipping round the wind-
ing Hollywood hill roads. Julie was
virtually the first of the other cast
members to arrive from New York.
Kazan had extensively recruited from
the Actors' Studio, and this influx of
New Yorkers must have helped miti-
gate Jimmy's restless boredom. Leonard
Rosenman and his wife also arrived.
On the recommendation of Leonard
Bernstein and Aaron Copland, Leonard
had been chosen to write the score for
East of Eden, his first film score. The
Rosenmans were almost a substitute
family for Jimmy and naturally he
had to show off his new love, the
MG. With both Rosenmans and
Gabrielle, their small daughter, in the
car he drove carefully, but later, driving

Leonard alone, he managed to spin off the road into some dustbins. Jimmy was suitably embarrassed and swore all who knew of the accident to secrecy.

On 26 May shooting of *East of Eden* commenced near Salinas, much of it acted out after hearing Rosenman's score so as to set the mood. This was how Prokofiev and Eisenstein had worked. Jimmy became very tired during shooting of the film due partly to partying late with, for example, the Rosenmans, and through dating a string of short-term girl-friends. He had always been something of an insomniac, which was worsened by his nervousness during shooting, and would spend the small hours driving around. Filming moved back to Hollywood after a week or two, and here Jimmy made a new friend, Lew Bracker, an insurance salesman, who was into the same things as Jimmy: girls and speed. He also met Marlon Brando again – they had encountered each other in New York. Jimmy revered Brando, but this was not reciprocated – Brando seemed to regard Jimmy as a pale imitation of himself. Years later he testified to Jimmy's talents as an actor, with the proviso that these were not as yet fully developed. Jimmy's closest friend in the cast was Julie Harris, who went out of her way to adjust to his performance, to such an extent that Kazan thought Jimmy could not have done *East of Eden* without her. The actor playing Cal's father was Raymond

Massey, a cultured traditional actor, who thought actors should read their lines as they were told to, and that they should always be ready when they were called on. Kazan played up to the difference between the two men in a scene where Cal's father was supposed to explode with rage by having Jimmy blaspheme outrageously while reading from the Bible. Sure enough Massey reacted in the way Kazan expected.

The biggest romance of Jimmy's life started at this time. The object of his love was Pier Angeli, a twenty-two-year-old actress from Sardinia, who had a part in *The Silver Chalice*, a film with a biblical theme (in which Paul Newman was the star – it was his first role in Hollywood, too, and he was one of Jimmy's acquaintances). Jimmy had met her on an evening out with Paul Newman. Jimmy was definitely 'hep', the word then for trendy, and this was a quality that the innocent and pure-looking Pier was fascinated by. The set of *The Silver Chalice* was adjacent to that of *East of Eden* and the two future lovers began to spend much of their time visiting each other. Kazan approved, in that it kept Jimmy out of his car and at the studio. Mrs Pierangeli (Pier's real name was Anna Maria Pierangeli) disapproved thoroughly – Jimmy was not a Catholic nor was he remotely presentable. The couple had to resort to subterfuge to disguise their continuing romance; Jimmy began to take more care over his appearance and to worry over what the press might say about him. But Mrs Pierangeli was no fool and took to changing her phone number so that Jimmy couldn't talk to Pier. This really upset Jimmy, who seemed very serious about Pier – they had even exchanged gold 'friendship' rings – and he had to resort to pleading with his friends to find out her number. Marriage was seriously on his mind.

At the same time their relationship was increasingly tempestuous. He was living on the lot next to Kazan, who often heard Pier and Jimmy rowing. After these rows Jimmy would get drunk and on one such occasion he rolled into a party at the Rosenmans to announce that Leonard was having an

James Dean greatly admired Marlon Brando

Off set with Natalie Wood

affair; whether Adele knew or not, Rosenman was justifiably incensed and after speaking his mind to Jimmy the next morning, the two were to stay out of contact for over a year. Jimmy had a strong self-destructive streak, especially tragic given his need for companionship. He became increasingly narcissistic, taking hundreds of photos of himself and trying to get Kazan to say which he preferred.

As soon as filming ended Kazan wanted Jimmy off the lot – he was simply far too disruptive. Apart from his usual antics, he had bought a new, larger, noisier motorcycle, a Triumph 500. It proved quite difficult to find a landlord or landlady who would take Jimmy, given his nocturnal habits, which included beating his bongos to calm himself down. He ended up in Dick Clayton's flat, which he referred to as a 'wastebasket with walls'.

Meanwhile, the director Nicholas Ray had approached Warner Bros with a proposal for a film about juvenile delinquency. Ray was fresh from directing *Johnny Guitar*, which had been a great success, and Warners were glad to support this new project. Initially Ray's film was to be entitled *Blind Run*, but Warners had the rights to a book called *Rebel Without a Cause*, whose screenplay had been rejected, and Ray was able to adopt the title. He started to work on his screenplay with Leon Uris (now a well-known author) but, after an argument, Uris was replaced by Irving Shulman. The two men worked for three months on the script.

Jimmy now returned to New York where Jane Deacy had got him a part in a TV show. He left in the almost certain knowledge that Pier Angeli was pregnant. He gave her an ultimatum to come with him to New York if she loved him, but she rejected this so as not to hurt her mother. In New York he bought baby clothes and sent them to Pier, with whom he seemed obsessed. Then, a bolt from the blue, it was announced that Pier would marry Vic Damone, an actor/singer she had known previously. Jimmy tried constantly to phone her but she refused to answer his calls. Jimmy was distraught and desperately sought solace from friends such as Christine White. After the TV show Jimmy returned to LA.

Rebel

Back in LA Jimmy met Natalie Wood, his future co-star in *Rebel Without a Cause* who worked with him on a TV show there. Jimmy did not seem particularly taken by Natalie or the show, ignoring her and arriving late for rehearsals, as always, on his motorcycle. He was still deeply affected by the ending of his affair with Pier, who was to be married in November. Jimmy wasn't invited to the wedding but watched the newlyweds come out of the church from his motorcycle, on which he noisily rode off.

Jimmy began to spend a lot of time with a group calling itself 'The Night Watch', one of whose luminaries was Maila Nurmi, a keen occultist, who introduced some TV 'horror' shows (by modern lights they would probably be regarded as comedy) as 'Vampyra'. One member of her entourage drove around in a hearse, which was regarded as eccentric. This group of insomniacs, including Jimmy, would cruise round Hollywood through the night drifting from one of the few open cafés to another. When not doing this he would call up friends, such as Eartha Kitt, in the middle of

As Jett Rink in *Giant*

The fatal drive in the Porsche

the night and ask them to go for rides with him. He also went to 'drum' parties, where a group of friends would gather with their drums and hammer their way into the night.

Jimmy went back to Fairmount for Christmas 1954, before returning to New York. There he joined up with Schatt who wanted to get a photo-essay on Jimmy into *Life* magazine. Jimmy was very much a participant in the essay, deciding how he wanted to look. This series, of pictures, though not published in *Life* magazine – *East of Eden* had as not yet been released, so Jimmy was not yet famous – became known as the 'Torn Sweater' series, as Jimmy's clothes were in their usual disreputable state, with a rent in his sweater, almost proto-'grunge'. He also bumped into Barbara Glenn for the last time; mutual sexual attraction was still there, but apparently they had nothing to say to each other. After they had made love, she told him she was getting married and left. That was the end of the relationship. It was almost as if Jimmy was visiting his old friends to tie up loose ends, to say goodbye. Jimmy spent a gloomy New Year's Eve at Schatt's studio, refusing to join in any merrymaking, instead miserably playing his bongos and casting his pall over everybody else.

In early 1955 he went on to make a TV programme in which the other actors complained that he mumbled

THEY DIED TOO YOUNG

his lines – this had been a common complaint with Brando, too. Bogart, for one, thought that there was a new 'mumbling' school. Furthermore, Jimmy did not always act predictably, and this confused many older actors throughout his career. He was intrinsically difficult, but also he wanted to add realism to his portrayal of characters; if you wanted a fellow actor not to act confused but to *be* confused then not doing what was expected was as good a way as any of achieving this. But at the same time it caused some irritation.

On 4 January 1955, it was announced that Jimmy had been signed up for *Rebel Without a Cause*. Jimmy returned to Los

Angeles. While on one of his late-
night cruises, he ran into Barbara
Hutton, the forty-three-year old
Woolworth's heiress. He turned on
all his charm for her, including a few
cock-and-bull stories about the jobs
he had done as an out-of-work actor.
The seduction technique worked and
he ended up chauffeuring her back to
her hotel on the back of his motorbike – he liked to test people's nerves
with a bit of speed – where he stayed
the night, perhaps the most extraordinary of his one-night stands! He
also won over Hedda Hopper, the
doyenne of Hollywood columnists,
though in a different way. He had
been introduced to her several
months earlier by the Warner Bros
publicity machine. She had not been

The scene of the crash

The grave of a legend

enamoured by Jimmy's laid-back
scruffy manner – she was very prop-
er – and had initially turned down an
invitation to the preview of *East of
Eden*. But one of her friends persuaded her it was worth seeing and
she was converted. She invited Jimmy for an interview and he turned up
precisely as she would have liked,
neat and presentable, the image of
a clean-living boy. He claimed that
the reason for his previous appearance as a 'bum' had been to see if she
had the courage to tell the truth about
him. This flattery worked and Hopper
said she'd like to be of help to him if
possible. Jimmy stated afterwards to
his friend, the journalist Joe Hyams,
that if he was natural with the press,
he only damaged his own reputation,

and Hopper would be a useful ally against the rest of the press. This was quite perceptive.

Nicholas Ray was now on his third scriptwriter for *Rebel Without a Cause*, Stewart Stern, a friend of Arthur Loew Jun, the producer. On 18 January production meetings began, and Jimmy found Ray to be sensitive and understanding, indulgent even. He was also a great drinker and party-giver and at one of his parties Jimmy met Dennis Stock, a freelance photographer from New York, who was in Los Angeles to find work, not because he liked Hollywood – he was totally unimpressed by the glitz, just as Jimmy was, when not the centre of attention. After Stock had seen Jimmy in *East of*

Eden – at the end of which the audience, including himself, clapped – he suggested to Ray that he embark on a photo-essay on Jimmy, but set in Fairmount, the town in which Jimmy was moulded. By offering an exclusive, he managed to persuade *Life* magazine to fund the exercise.

The pair set off for Fairmount via New York. Jimmy saw such friends as Christine White and Eartha Kitt, while Stock took informal photos of him. This series of photos provides many of the images of Jimmy with which we are now familiar. He also went to see Dizzy Sheridan. They went to a party but Jimmy was in such a foul mood that the other guests all left. Afterwards he said goodbye to her. Arlene Sachs had a new boyfriend and, despite his saying to Jimmy when they met, 'They say you gave head to get ahead', Jimmy and he afterwards got on well enough. Barbara Glenn, his early passion, was now engaged to the director Mark Gordon, whom Jimmy insisted on meeting. Surprisingly he didn't create a scene. It was as if he wanted to say to all the women in his past that he was leaving their lives, and was giving his blessing. It may have been because of some inkling of his impending doom, but as likely it was his sense that he was moving into a bigger world. At his last meeting with Rogers Brackett, who wanted to borrow money off him after losing his job, he refused unless the money was signed for which, if businesslike, was hard, as Jimmy had certainly not signed for all the money he had borrowed off Brackett in the past. Also he told Brackett that he no longer needed him and his 'fairy' friends.

Stock and Jimmy then flew to Fairmount, and here Stock was able to see Jimmy in his original environment. Jimmy changed into his farmboy gear as soon as he got back. Stock took another series of photos showing Jimmy, including some at the Fairmount High School Valentine's dance, where Jimmy was pleased to be the centre of adulation. Jimmy also insisted that Stock take some photos of him in a coffin, partly because he knew that Sarah Bernhardt had done so, and partly just to find out what it was like; it was his strange urge to push out the borders of experience. Naturally, Fairmount town was scandalized by what it regarded as this extraordinary behaviour, apart from Marcus Winslow who was philosophical – after all, he had brought Jimmy up and knew his eccentricities of old. Stock's photos were then published in *Life*, after initial resistance – they were used to glamour shots – under the title 'Moody New Star'.

Jimmy then returned to New York, where Nick Ray joined him, to look for other members of the cast for *Rebel Without a Cause*. While he was in New York Warner signed up Jimmy for the part of Jett Rink in *Giant*, to be directed by George Stevens. Jimmy then left

New York, on 7 March, the day before the première preview of *East of Eden* in Times Square, saying he 'couldn't handle that scene', meaning the saccharine host of stars who had come to attend, and who would have doubtless afterwards oozed with unctuous congratulations. *Rebel* was due to begin filming at the end of March.

In Los Angeles again, he took comfort in the arms of Lilli Kardell, a Swedish starlet, who kept a comprehensive diary, including asterisks to show when she had made love! Jimmy had now bought his first Porsche, a 'Super Speedster', and he gave lifts in this and on his motorbike to Stern, who was putting the finishing touches to the script. Given what this did to Stern's nerves, it's amazing he actually finished it. Stern had condensed all the action into one day, and included knife-fights and high-speed 'chicken' runs (as in the 1973 film *American Graffiti*). The plot centred on teenage gangs, alienated from their unloving or absent parents, trying to find their own identity; Jimmy was almost typecast. A real gang leader was included among the extras to make sure that the action was authentic – the only condition was that he, and the other teenagers, had to be shorter than Jimmy, i.e. less than 5 feet 8 inches! Natalie Wood, despite her innocent appearance, and the fact that she was only seventeen (Warner Bros didn't like hiring minors as they had to attend lessons at the studio), got the female lead. Just before filming began, though, Jimmy got cold feet and fled back to New York. He wanted to work under Kazan again, with whom he had established a good working relationship. Stern had to choose his words carefully to get Jimmy to come back.

Just before shooting began Jimmy entered the Palm Springs Road Races. He wanted to try out the 'Super Speedster'. Initially the other competitors thought of him as a joke, a film star amateur just there to beef up his image. But Jimmy qualified for the second day's races and came second overall. According to another driver, though, he was a real danger on the track: 'He wanted to win too much and would take any kind of chance to be first.'

After *Rebel* began shooting Ray was called in by Warner Bros executives who simply couldn't understand the sort of film that was being made. Ray threatened to quit and they caved in. They also decided to shoot the film in colour which was Ray's preferred medium, although it meant redoing scenes that had already been shot. Jimmy and Ray by now got on well; Ray let Jimmy improvise and when he wanted things done differently he would talk to an actor or actress individually and suggest it, rather than bawl out instructions.

Meanwhile *East of Eden* had opened in Los Angeles, and Jimmy became famous overnight. The reaction of American teenagers, who at last had a star they could identify with, was way beyond Warner's expectations and fan clubs were formed all over the USA. He was mobbed in all his favourite haunts. Like many emotionally troubled people, Jimmy found it too much; although he had always wanted to be the centre of attention, the sheer quantity of attention – the fact that one could never escape it, that people were hanging on one's every word – was overwhelming, and he resumed seeing a psychoanalyst. He needed to have the demons inside him quietened down. His dreams and insomnia were getting worse.

Giant had now begun filming in Virginia where Stevens heard that Jimmy had entered another race, the Santa

Barbara Road Races. Unlike Ray
who thought it good for Jimmy to
have an outlet of his own, where he
could be successful on his own account,
Stevens was worried about his valuable
property and banned Jimmy from racing until the filming of *Giant* was over.
This didn't stop Jimmy ordering a
Lotus IX in his search for more
speed, nor from driving manically in
the hills behind Hollywood. The film
crew of *Giant* moved to the West, to
the small town of Marfa, and Jimmy
began shooting on 3 June. This was his
first big-name film as Elizabeth Taylor
and Rock Hudson were also starring.
Dennis Hopper was in it, too, but as a
new face. But Stevens and Jimmy
didn't get on very well – there was a
conflict of wills, even though Jimmy

was to admit that Stevens was getting a good performance out of him. Eventually he called his old friend Rod Steiger, who had been at the Actors' Studio in the old New York days, and Steiger was able to calm him down a little. Despite Jimmy's confrontational attitude, he also wanted to please Stevens and was eventually able to do so, during the 'Last Supper' scene, when he had to play Jett Rink at 46. He hadn't been playing the scene particularly well and finally asked Stevens' advice, after which he performed immaculately. This rapprochement pleased Jimmy greatly.

In August Pier Angeli had her baby, a boy. Damone bumped into Jimmy and Lew Bracker in a restaurant, asked them to drink a toast to his son. Jimmy apparently did so, but after Damone had left said, 'I'll drink a toast to *my* son anytime.' Apparently Damone was never sure of the boy's paternity either. But Jimmy was much more excited about another arrival: he traded in his 'Super Speedster' for a Porsche 550, a 'Spyder' which was significantly faster, if rather more un-stable. He then drove the car to the lot to show off to all his friends. Appar-ently many were uneasy, seeing him in a vehicle which barely reached above his knee when he stood beside it, it was so low. It was silver too, which made it almost invisible. But shooting for Giant had finished and Jimmy wanted to go racing again, and this was the machine to do it in, or so he thought. Ironically, given what was about to happen, and his terrorization of the studio lot in or on his various means of transport, he made a road safety film. Luckily for his estate though, Bracker, who was also an insurance salesman, as well as a fellow boy racer, had got Jimmy to take out a $100,000 policy on his life. Jimmy also had the number '130' painted on the car and the words 'Little Bastard' on the rear.

He left for Salinas, the home of Monty Roberts, to race his new toy. He had asked several of his friends, and even his father, if they would accompany him on the trip but they were all unable to. Originally the plan had been to tow the car on a trailer, but Jimmy decided to drive it with his mechanic, presumably to get to know it better and to loosen it up, as it was still a new car. On the way to Salinas, Jimmy and the follow-up car with the trailer were booked for speeding. This didn't deter Jimmy as he resumed the journey to Salinas, agreeing to meet his escort at Paso Robles, 150 miles up Route 466. At about 5 o'clock he bumped into an acquaintance, Lance Reventlow, the son of Barbara Hutton, on the way to the races in his gull-wing Mercedes, and boasted to him that he had had 130 on the clock. Bill Hickman, in the escort car, warned him to slow down – it was early evening and the Porsche was not a highly visible machine. But Jimmy just laughed this off, before racing back out on to the highway.

About half an hour later the Porsche was approaching the 'Y' junction between Routes 466 and 41, a notorious blackspot. Jimmy overtook one witness at a speed of at least 85 mph, and maybe much more. A Ford saloon drew on to the highway. A collision was inevitable. The tiny Porsche smashed into the Ford and virtually demolished itself. The jaw and femur of the race mechanic, Rolf Weutherich, were broken. Jimmy had 'a broken neck, multiple broken bones and lacerations' according to the doctor's report. He had been almost decapitated, and was certified 'Dead on Arrival' at the Paso Robles War

Memorial Hospital. So, in a way, a legend died and so, in a way, a legend was born.